Lovey Dovey

a children's book about connection,
love, peace, and giving

ISBN 979-8-89526-025-8 (paperback)
ISBN 979-8-89345-475-8 (hardcover)
ISBN 979-8-89345-476-5 (digital)

Christian Faith Publishing
832 Park Avenue
Meadville, PA 16335
www.christianfaithpublishing.com

Illustrations by Coiler Vopaer

Printed in the United States of America

Lovey Dovey

a children's book about connection,
love, peace, and giving

Gabrielle Fisher

Manny the mouse felt lonely one day.

He looked for his friends to play.

They weren't around, so he felt down.

He slumped and grumped that day.

He went outside to ask the sky,
"Where is the love and why?"
The sun shone bright and within sight,
a dove came swooping by.

4

His name was Lovey Dovey
with his feathers so sleek and white.
He was filled with love and peace,
and was shiny as a light.

Lovey Dovey heard the call
that Manny needed a friend,
and as quick as a flash,
Lovey Dovey did dash
to help his heartbreak end.

Lovey Dovey was wise and good.
He always had more to give.
Lovey Dovey loved everybody
because giving was how he lived.

Lovey Dovey said to Manny,
"Why are you so glum?"
Manny looked at him and said,
"There is no one around to make a sound
and I am feeling kind of numb."

Lovey Dovey said to Manny,
"Look inside your heart of hearts,
there is a little light.
This light brings love and joy thereof
and takes away the fright."

So when you're feeling lonely,
quiet your mind and look inside,
and remember what I say,

"Love is the thing
that will make you sing and your
sadness will go away."

When Lovey Dovey said these things,
Manny knew the truth.
He felt joy and said, "Oh boy,
my heartbreak is cut loose!"

Manny was filled with gratitude
for the message the Dove did give him.
And when it was told, the truth of old,
the love was all within him.

You too can be wise
and good and kind
when you give this love away.
So make yourself clear and bright,
then give this peace and love and light
to everyone each day.

We want to be kind and with this in mind, share this light with others.
To make it grow, we let it flow to all our sisters and brothers.

Lovey Dovey was wise and good.
He always had more to give.
Lovey Dovey loved everybody
because giving was how he lived.

About the Author

Gabrielle Fisher is an occupational therapist and the owner of Fisher Therapeutics in Knoxville, Tennessee. For over twenty years, she has worked with people of all ages to improve their health and well-being. As this world is getting more complicated, she felt a calling to help children and their families remember to rely on God's love and grace to live a life filled with integrity and virtue. She hopes you experience the beauty, fun, and empowerment of these sweet stories.

www.ingramcontent.com/pod-product-compliance
Lightning Source LLC
Chambersburg PA
CBHW040315170225
22013CB00042B/176